A Journal FOR Family CAREGIVERS

Your Place for Thoughts, Plans, and Dreams

HARRIET HODGSON

Georgia

A Journal for Family Caregivers: Your Place for Thoughts, Plans, and Dreams

Published in the United States by WriteLife Publishing
(An imprint of Boutique of Quality Books Publishing Company)
www.writelife.com

Printed in the United States of America.
Library of Congress Control Number: 2015948522

978-1-60808-150-9 (p)
978-1-60808-151-6 (e)

Book design by Robin Krauss, www.bookformatters.com
Cover photo from www.istockphoto.com
Cover Design by Ellis Dixon

For more information about Harriet Hodgson please visit www.harriethodgson.com or send an email to harriethodgson@charter.net.

CONTENTS

FOREWORD
What Makes This Journal Different?

Dozens of journals are available today. There are gratitude journals, knitting journals, walking journals, weather journals, bird watching journals, and more; the list goes on and on. With so many journals available, why choose this one? Six features make this journal stand out from the crowd. Each feature is important and designed to help you.

This journal is for family caregivers. The topics in this journal are ones you deal with all the time: completing caregiving tasks, getting through a day, taking care of your own health, monitoring positive and negative self-talk, dealing with emotions, and more. You will recognize the topics the minute you see them. In fact, you may find yourself saying, "I know about this one." Because the journal is designed for you—a family caregiver—you can "settle" into it quickly. Use the journal to record facts, special events, new ideas, challenges, and dreams.

It isn't a diary. A diary calls for a rather formal kind of writing and requires daily entries, something you may not have time for right now. In contrast, a journal invites a casual form of writing that requires *consistent* entries. Consistent is the word to remember. You may write every other day, every few days, every week, every other week—whatever works for you. Not having to write daily can be motivating, and you may find yourself writing more than you thought you would.

The journal contains affirmations. An affirmation can set the tone for your caregiving day. You may wish to copy the affirmation on a small piece of paper and stick it in your pocket. The affirmations in this journal come directly from my caregiving life. I've been a family caregiver for three generations—caring for my mother, my twin grandchildren, and my husband—so I understand your caregiving life. I also understand some of the challenges you face. Caregiving is an expanding role, and this journal can help you track new tasks.

The prompts are different. Before I started writing this journal, I looked at sample journals and read books and articles about journaling. With a couple of exceptions, all of the journals I found used questions as writing prompts. I can't speak for you, but I have enough questions in my life, and I don't need any more. This journal starts a sentence for you and allows you to finish it; writing is easy because you have a jump-start. Before you know it, you may have written several paragraphs.

Each page ends with action steps. Look for the Action heading at the bottom of each page. This is the proactive part of your journal: a place for your To-Do lists, grocery lists, supply lists, and issues you need to consider and act upon. If no action is required, write "no action required" or "continue existing plan" or "brainstorm on action steps." Although you may be tempted to leave this space blank, I hope you use it.

You have options. Maybe you don't like the page topic and prefer to write about another one—that's okay. Just cross out the topic and insert the one you want to write about. After all, this is YOUR journal, and you may use it as you wish. When the journal is full, write the beginning and ending dates on the title page and put it away. Begin another journal and discover more about your caregiving journey, one of the most challenging and unique journeys of life. Happy journaling!

You wind up with an action plan. At the end of the daily entry you have listed some action steps. When you reach the end of the journal, you have created a Caregiving Action Plan. This plan can make your life, and your loved one's life, easier.

INTRODUCTION

I didn't get up one day and mutter to myself, "It's been a slow week. I think I'll write a journaling book." Instead, this resource comes from my extensive caregiving experience, starting with my mother. She had dementia, the result of a series of mini strokes. Although my mother lived in an assisted living community, I was involved in her life and did something for her every day. Caring for my mother was a journey of its own.

Every Sunday, I cooked a gourmet dinner for her. Mondays and Tuesdays were usually errand days. I took her out to lunch on Wednesdays at a variety of restaurants. But my mother's dementia became so bad I changed the plan and took her to the same restaurant. This worked until my mother started looking around nervously and asking, "How the hell do you get out of this place?" From then on, I asked the hostess to seat us near the door to calm my mother's anxiety.

Thursdays and Fridays were health care days. I arranged for medical and dental visits, and I drove her to the appointments and stayed with her while she was there. Saturdays were catch-up days, and we did whatever needed to be done—shopping for clothes, buying Christmas gifts, or walking around the mall. Finally, the day I dreaded came, the day when my mother didn't recognize me. This changed my caregiving role to a patient advocate's role. I attended patient conferences, arranged for extra baths, continued to have my mother over for dinner, and visited her until she died.

My caregiving days were so busy I had become exhausted. Nine years of caregiving depleted my physical reserves, and it took me a year to regain my energy. It was a good thing because there was more caregiving to do. On a snowy Friday in February of 2007, my elder daughter died from the injuries she received in a car crash. Surgeons operated on her for twenty hours but were unable to save her life. Two days later, on Sunday, my father-in-law succumbed to pneumonia at age ninety-eight. Although I anticipated his death, the finality of it still came as a shock. Two months later, my brother and only sibling died of a heart attack. What a roller coaster of emotions.

I would start to feel better, and then another family member would die. In the fall of 2007, my twin grandchildren's father died in another car crash. The county court appointed my husband and me as their guardians and financial conservators.

The twins (one boy, one girl) were fifteen years old when they moved in with us. My husband and I divided our duties. I was in charge of the house and school issues, and he handled estate documents and finances. Although teenagers hadn't changed much since our daughters were teens, some changes had taken place. I had to figure out a way to grieve for four family members while caring for two vulnerable children. Then, and now, I decided that love would be my guide. I based my caregiving decisions on what was best for my grandchildren.

The twins graduated from high school with honors. In 2014, after living with us for seven years, they graduated from college with highest honors, Phi Beta Kappa, and additional honors. Unfortunately, my husband was unable to attend their graduations, so I observed the ceremonies extra carefully for both of us and had to fight back tears many times. Although many new college graduates have been unable to get jobs, both of the twins found jobs they enjoyed. They now live in my hometown of Rochester, Minnesota, and come for dinner every other Sunday. I am blessed to have them in my life.

Now I am my husband's family caregiver, a role I never envisioned. In October of 2013, my husband's aorta split like a garden hose. I drove him to the hospital Emergency Department, only ten minutes away and, according to one of the nurses, arrived "just in time". John was bleeding to death, and the health care team pumped blood into him as fast as they could. Unfortunately, the internal bleeding didn't stop, and my husband agreed to life-threatening surgery. The surgeons saved his life, but he suffered a spinal stroke during the operation, and it paralyzed his legs.

He was hospitalized for eight long months before finally being dismissed to my care. While he was in the hospital, I cleaned out our tri-level home, listed it with a realtor, and built a wheelchair-friendly townhome, where we live now. It was an emotional, gut-wrenching, and lonely experience. Caring for my disabled husband is probably the biggest challenge of my life. Caregiving is physically and emotionally taxing, yet I try to stay cheerful and upbeat.

As I have done so often, I turned to my occupation—freelance writing—for comfort and understanding. Because I'm a nonfiction writer, I'm constantly researching topics and learning in the process. Writing turned out to be a wise decision and led to my series of books on caregiving: *The Family Caregiver's Guide, Affirmations for Family Caregivers*, and this journal. The decision to write about caregiving has also produced many articles on the topic.

People often ask me if I keep a journal, and my answer is negative. Whether they are about grief healing, family caregiving, or self-care, the books and articles I write serve as my journals. I didn't plan this; it just happened. But I strongly recommend journaling or writing down your thoughts and feelings for every caregiver. To keep a journal you don't have to be a writer like me. Anyone can do it. Willingness, a pen or pencil, and the ability to string words together in sentences are all you need. If you don't feel like writing sentences, write a few descriptive words. Journaling has many caregiving benefits, which are detailed in the next chapter.

Chapter 1

Benefits of Journaling

Journaling has so many benefits that the topic could be a book by itself. This chapter focuses on some of the key benefits. Keeping a journal is a form of self-care, and over time, it can literally change your life. You may begin to see things that weren't apparent before. Themes, patterns, and symbols may start to emerge. Feelings you didn't realize you had are expressed in your words. Although you're the person keeping the journal, you may surprise yourself.

You get to know you. Journal writing is a way to explore your identity. Your handwriting (whether good or bad) and the words you choose aren't nearly as important as the thoughts behind your words. A year from now, when you go back and read your journal, you may find yourself thinking, *I handled that pretty well.* Page-by-page, a detailed picture of you emerges from the journal. You may also see a picture of the love that sustains you.

Journaling is a form of self-care and support. Kathleen Adams, M.A., in her book, *Journal to the Self: Twenty-Two Paths to Personal Growth,* describes journaling as a bridge to humanity and spirituality (p. xv). A therapist herself, Adams refers to her personal journal as her seventy-nine-cent therapist. As she explains, "Your journal can serve as a magic mirror into which you can gaze and see reflected back to you the various parts of yourself" (16). One page at a time, journaling helps you learn and cope.

Your journal is an historical document. The words you write detail your caregiving journey and also document family history. Years from now, a grandchild may wonder how you got through this time and will decide to read your journal. Other family members, ones who live far away, may be interested in the journal as well. What seems ordinary to you may be important to succeeding generations. For this reason alone, I encourage you to make journal entries even when you don't feel like it. If you're rushed, jot down a few words that describe your feelings, such as *tired, anxious,* and *encouraged.* As Christina Baldwin writes in her book, *One to One: Self-Understanding Through Journal Writing,* "What we leave in the journal is a code, a hint, the story of things which help us recall . . ." (p. 6).

You see the scope of caregiving. Until you expressed your ideas in words, you may not have been aware of the expanding role of caregiving. Reading past journal entries can clarify your caregiving mission and the tasks associated with it. You may also become aware of the secondary tasks associated with your primary tasks. For example, driving your loved one to the doctor is secondary to making an appointment with her or his physician. Secondary tasks can take more time than the initial ones.

You activate your writing ability. Journaling can make a writer out of anyone. Although you may think of yourself as a word klutz, keeping a journal can help you frame better sentences, use words you haven't used in months, expand your vocabulary, describe experiences poetically, and write from the heart. All of these things are possible when you keep a journal. However, you have to allow enough time for writing skills to develop. Months from now, when you put this journal away, you may be surprised at the creative writing within its pages.

Journaling can be an emotional release. You can fool yourself for a while, but the words you choose and the things you describe will eventually reveal your feelings. For example, you may not realize how frustrated you are until you have read some of your journal entries. Uncomfortable emotions, such as anger, may also be revealed in the journal pages. It's wise to identify your feelings if you can: disappointment, worry, sadness, encouragement, happiness, excitement, etc.

Writing can help you problem-solve. As you make entries, you may become aware of problems. But as you read more, you may come to realize that things aren't as bad as you thought. More importantly, solutions to your problems may start to appear. The Action section of the journaling page can help you explore solutions. You can pick the best solution and start working on it. Although your solutions may not appear instantly, they are somewhere in your writing.

Entries increase your power of observation. Just the fact that you're keeping a journal makes you more observant of your loved one and the care you provide. Journaling may become the lens through which you view life. As Christina Baldwin writes in *One to One*, "We are capable of having a relationship with our own minds" (p. 9). She goes on to say that these acts of observing and writing about what we observe are a duality of the conscious mind.

Have worries about privacy kept you from journaling? There are steps you can take to protect your privacy. Start by writing on the first page of this journal, "DO NOT READ. THIS DOCUMENT IS PRIVATE." You may keep your journal in a locked drawer or a home safe. When you are finished with the journal, protect your privacy by storing it in a bank safe deposit box. Journal entries that are kept on a computer may be password-protected. Don't let worry stop you from reaping the benefits of journaling.

Chapter 2

Journaling Tips for You

One of the best things about journaling is that there are no hard-and-fast rules. You may write stream of consciousness thoughts (also called flow writing), record nighttime dreams, answer questions (a dialoge with yourself), tell true stories, develop a theme, reminisce about life, enter detailed descriptions, explain your views, describe a process, add drawings to journal pages, or write poetry. Write to understand and empower yourself.

The following tips will help you fill your journal from cover to cover.

- **Choose the best writing tool.** It should be something you're comfortable with: a favorite pen, felt-tip pen, drawing pen, pencil, or colored pencils. Whichever writing instrument you choose, make sure it glides and allows you to write quickly.
- **Cast grammar, punctuation, and spelling aside.** Your goal is to get words on paper, not to win a language contest. Even if you have good grammar, punctuation, and spelling skills, this isn't the time to focus on such things.
- **Don't worry about handwriting.** Again, your goal is to get words on paper. If your handwriting is really illegible, you may wish to print. In addition to this journal, you may keep one on your computer.

- **Try to write at the same time each day.** When you do this, you are more apt to make ongoing entries. Take advantage of your high-energy times. If early morning is a high-energy time for you, this may be a good time to write. Or you may wish to write after dinner when things quiet down a bit. Choose a time that's conducive to your schedule, a time that inspires you to write.
- **Choose a good writing place.** Although many people are able to write amidst the noise and bustle of a coffee shop, you may not be one of them. To foster writing, find a quiet place and sit in a comfortable chair. You want to be able to "hear" your innermost thoughts.
- **Be quiet for a few minutes.** You may meditate or say a prayer. Hard as it may be, try to clear your mind of clutter before you start writing. A quiet lead-in will make writing easier. Your thoughts may be clearer too.
- **Begin writing.** Stress management expert Elizabeth Scott, M.S., author of the article "The Benefits of Journaling: How to Get Started," posted on About.com, thinks it's best to just begin writing. "Don't think about what to say," she advises, "just begin writing, and the words should come."
- **Make ongoing entries**. Try to write regularly, every few days or every other week. If this isn't possible, don't worry, and write when you can. You may simply complete the sentence prompt and leave it at that.
- **Write for 5 minutes or more.** If you're short of time, write for five minutes or so. You don't have to write paragraphs. Some people choose to keep one-sentence journals, and this approach may suit you. However, you will get more from your journal if you write more.
- **Borrow ideas from others.** In her PsychCentral website article, "Tips to Start Journaling," Margarita Tartakovsky, M.S., says you may copy song lyrics, quotations, or lines from an inspiring poem into your journal.

- **Tuck mementos in your journal.** This idea comes from April Rogers, author of the article "Journal Writing Tips," posted on the Scribe Time website. Tucking mementos in your journal—a note, photo, theater program, pressed flower—makes your journal more meaningful.
- **Prepare for slack time.** Christina Baldwin thinks ignoring writing comes with the journaling territory. "It happens for one reason or another," she explains, and her solution is to "simply start again" (p. 33). This takes willpower, and you have that power within you.
- **Review your entries.** Kathleen Adams, author of *Journal to the Self*, suggests giving each review about thirty minutes. Don't rush this process. Take the time to read your entries and understand their meaning. "Your notes will jog your memory and enable you to summarize your daily activities and discoveries," Adams explains (p. 164).
- **Let your journal lead you.** Your journal entries may cause you to research a topic, change direction, ask family members for help, seek outside help, revise your daily routine, or start planning a future. Many productive things can come from journaling.

Chapter 3

How to Use This Journal

Before you start writing, look at a sample page and notice its structure. At the top there is a place for the **date**. It's important to date every entry to understand the context of your writing. The date is followed by a **one-sentence affirmation**, encouraging words that may help you center your thoughts. A **writing prompt**—the beginning of a sentence—comes next, and you finish the sentence any way you choose. Some examples of prompts are:

> *The happiest part of this day . . .*
>
> *How I wish . . .*
>
> *I'm concerned about . . .*
>
> *When I'm discouraged, I . . .*
>
> *I feel like crying when . . .*
>
> *I express my love by . . .*
>
> *Friends tell me . . .*
>
> *I'm surprised at . . .*
>
> *I feel helpless when . . .*

Writing lines come after the prompt. There should be enough space for you to record your thoughts. If you need more space, tuck a piece of lined paper into the journal and continue writing. Long entries, paragraphs that fill two pages or more, may become a computer file.

The last heading on the page is **Action.** This is a place for brainstorming: let your thoughts wander, make lists, explore proactive steps, and make plans. The value of this section will become apparent as you use it. Here are some examples of planning sentences.

Learn more about my loved one's illness.

Include more "me time" in each day.

Call a friend and meet her (him) for coffee.

Sign up for a caregiving course.

Join a caregiving support group.

Keep a Caregiving Happiness Jar.

Visit an online caregiving community.

Make follow-up appointment with my loved one's physician.

When you come to the end of your journal, read all the things you wrote in the Action sections. Put a checkmark by the most important step on each page. This process may take several days. Use these steps to create an action plan for your loved one. You don't have to include all the steps in your plan, just the best ones. However, your plan should be realistic and workable for your loved one.

Discuss the plan with your loved one to help her or him feel in control. Your loved one may think of more planning ideas. Keep journaling. When one journal is full, start another one. Bind a year's worth of journals together and note the year. A new chapter of life awaits you, and it can be documented in your journal.

Katrina Kenison writes about journaling in her book, *The Gift of an Ordinary Day: A Mother's Memoir.* Kenison kept journals for years. As soon as a journal was finished, she tucked it away and didn't think of it again. Moving to a new place brought her in contact with her journals, which were packed away in boxes. Reading some entries brought her face-to-face with herself as a younger, solitary, questioning woman. "My journals tell a story that I never bothered to read," she writes. "Now, I see my soul has been hard at work in those pages." Kenison decided to celebrate her journals by paying attention to them and continuing her personal growth (p. 207–208).

You can do this too, so start your journal now.

Chapter 4

Journaling Pages

_____

DATE

AFFIRMATION

Self-care is part of my caregiving journey.

WRITING PROMPT

I care for myself by

_____

_____

_____

_____

_____

_____

_____

_____

_____

_____

_____

_____

ACTION

_____

_____

_____

_____

DATE

AFFIRMATION

Although getting enough sleep is a challenge,
I average seven hours a night.

WRITING PROMPT

Preparing for sleep is on my schedule, and each night I

_____

_____

_____

_____

_____

_____

_____

_____

_____

_____

_____

_____

ACTION

_____

_____

_____

_____

AFFIRMATION

My caregiving story is really a love story.

WRITING PROMPT

I show the love I feel for my loved one in many ways:

_____

_____

_____

_____

_____

_____

_____

_____

_____

_____

_____

_____

ACTION

_____

_____

_____

_____

DATE

AFFIRMATION

I am grateful for my caregiving support system.

WRITING PROMPT

Just checked my support system, and it needs

_____

_____

_____

_____

_____

_____

_____

_____

_____

_____

_____

_____

ACTION

_____

_____

_____

_____

AFFIRMATION

*Changes in plans don't throw me off balance;
they activate my coping skills.*

WRITING PROMPT

My coping skills include

_____

_____

_____

_____

_____

_____

_____

_____

_____

_____

_____

ACTION

_____

_____

_____

_____

_____

DATE

AFFIRMATION

*Caregiving boundaries provide structure for
my loved one and me.*

WRITING PROMPT

Some of my caregiving boundaries are

_____

_____

_____

_____

_____

_____

_____

_____

_____

_____

_____

_____

ACTION

_____

_____

_____

_____

DATE
_____

AFFIRMATION

Despite the sameness of caregiving days,
I bring originality to each one.

WRITING PROMPT

I demonstrate originality

_____

_____

_____

_____

_____

_____

_____

_____

_____

_____

ACTION

_____

_____

_____

_____

DATE

AFFIRMATION

*Impatience comes with the caregiving territory,
and I contain my impatience.*

WRITING PROMPT

I get impatient when

_____

_____

_____

_____

_____

_____

_____

_____

_____

_____

_____

ACTION

_____

_____

_____

_____

DATE

AFFIRMATION

I will always be part of my loved one's cheering section.

WRITING PROMPT

I cheer for my loved one's

_____

_____

_____

_____

_____

_____

_____

_____

_____

_____

_____

_____

ACTION

_____

_____

_____

_____

DATE

AFFIRMATION

Avoiding overly loud noise is a way to avoid stress.

WRITING PROMPT

To stay away from the stress mess, I

_____

_____

_____

_____

_____

_____

_____

_____

_____

_____

_____

ACTION

_____

_____

_____

_____

DATE

AFFIRMATION

*For my health and well-being, I choose to spend time
with upbeat, positive people.*

WRITING PROMPT

The positive people in my life are:

_____

_____

_____

_____

_____

_____

_____

_____

_____

_____

_____

ACTION

_____

_____

_____

_____

DATE

AFFIRMATION

Every caregiver feels overwhelmed now and then,
and I remind myself of this daily.

WRITING PROMPT

I feel overwhelmed

ACTION

DATE

AFFIRMATION

Laughter lifts my spirits and soothes my worries.

WRITING PROMPT

Many things make me laugh, including

_____

_____

_____

_____

_____

_____

_____

_____

_____

_____

_____

ACTION

_____

_____

_____

_____

DATE

AFFIRMATION

Asking for help isn't a sign of weakness; it is a reality check.

WRITING PROMPT

The reality of my caregiving life is

_____

_____

_____

_____

_____

_____

_____

_____

_____

_____

_____

_____

ACTION

_____

_____

_____

_____

AFFIRMATION

I feel blessed by the happy caregiving days I experience.

WRITING PROMPT

So many things make me happy:

_____

_____

_____

_____

_____

_____

_____

_____

_____

_____

_____

_____

ACTION

_____

_____

_____

_____

DATE

AFFIRMATION

Sometimes it feels like my loved one is taking care of me.

WRITING PROMPT

My loved one takes care of me

ACTION

DATE

AFFIRMATION

"No" is often a self-care word, one I use to defend
myself and my time.

WRITING PROMPT

I have to say "no" when

_____

_____

_____

_____

_____

_____

_____

_____

_____

_____

_____

ACTION

_____

_____

_____

_____

DATE

AFFIRMATION

Happy memories help me cope with the stress of caregiving.

WRITING PROMPT

Some of my happiest memories are

ACTION

AFFIRMATION

Positive thinking often requires effort, and that's okay with me.

WRITING PROMPT

I switch negative thinking to positive by

_____

_____

_____

_____

_____

_____

_____

_____

_____

_____

_____

_____

ACTION

_____

_____

_____

_____

AFFIRMATION

People say I'm their hero, but I'm simply someone who takes care of those I love.

WRITING PROMPT

Some of the ways I care for my loved one are:

_____

_____

_____

_____

_____

_____

_____

_____

_____

_____

_____

_____

ACTION

_____

_____

_____

_____

_____

AFFIRMATION

No matter what else is happening, each day has its happy moments,
some great, some small.

WRITING PROMPT

The happiest part of this day

_____

_____

_____

_____

_____

_____

_____

_____

_____

_____

ACTION

_____

_____

_____

_____

DATE

AFFIRMATION

*Caregiving has some sad moments, and I have learned
to accept them.*

WRITING PROMPT

I feel like crying when

ACTION

DATE

AFFIRMATION

Keeping a happiness jar filled with dated messages about happy experiences helps me see life positively and appreciate the life I have.

WRITING PROMPT

These are some sample notes from my happiness jar:

_____

_____

_____

_____

_____

_____

_____

_____

_____

_____

_____

ACTION

_____

_____

_____

_____

DATE

AFFIRMATION

My new caregiving job hasn't robbed me of my identity.

WRITING PROMPT

To retain and sustain my identity, I

ACTION

_____

AFFIRMATION

I try to give myself the gift of self-confidence each day.

WRITING PROMPT

Some of my self-confidence boosters are

_____

_____

_____

_____

_____

_____

_____

_____

_____

_____

_____

_____

ACTION

_____

_____

_____

_____

DATE
_____

AFFIRMATION

Well-meaning friends offer me advice and, although
I appreciate their concern, I ignore some of their ideas.

WRITING PROMPT

Friends tell me

_____

_____

_____

_____

_____

_____

_____

_____

_____

_____

_____

ACTION

_____

_____

_____

_____

AFFIRMATION

I accept the fact that I had to let go of some things
to become a family caregiver.

WRITING PROMPT

I had to let go of

_____

_____

_____

_____

_____

_____

_____

_____

_____

_____

_____

ACTION

_____

_____

_____

_____

AFFIRMATION

Essential supplies—a gentle spirit and heart—are always with me.

WRITING PROMPT

I activate my gentle spirit by

_____

_____

_____

_____

_____

_____

_____

_____

_____

_____

_____

ACTION

_____

_____

_____

_____

_____

AFFIRMATION

Although it has taken practice, I have learned to calm myself and my soul.

WRITING PROMPT

These are some of my calming steps:

_____

_____

_____

_____

_____

_____

_____

_____

_____

_____

_____

ACTION

_____

_____

_____

_____

_____

DATE

AFFIRMATION

Because color affects my mood I choose to wear happy colors.

WRITING PROMPT

The color that makes me happiest is

_____

_____

_____

_____

_____

_____

_____

_____

_____

_____

_____

ACTION

_____

_____

_____

_____

DATE

AFFIRMATION

*It's okay to wish for changes and things,
and I don't berate myself for doing it.*

WRITING PROMPT

How I wish

_____

_____

_____

_____

_____

_____

_____

_____

_____

_____

_____

ACTION

_____

_____

_____

_____

DATE

AFFIRMATION

Happiness is a choice, and I choose it for myself every day.

WRITING PROMPT

Today I choose to be happy because

ACTION

_____

AFFIRMATION

Caregiving has its physical demands, and rather than complaining about them, I view them as ways to stay fit.

WRITING PROMPT

The biggest physical demand of my caregiving is

_____

_____

_____

_____

_____

_____

_____

_____

_____

_____

_____

ACTION

_____

_____

_____

_____

DATE

AFFIRMATION

Having a ready sense of humor can save a caregiving day.

WRITING PROMPT

Many things make me laugh:

_____

_____

_____

_____

_____

_____

_____

_____

_____

_____

_____

_____

ACTION

_____

_____

_____

_____

DATE

AFFIRMATION

Taking time to know myself makes me a better caregiver.

WRITING PROMPT

Journaling is helping me know myself better

_____

_____

_____

_____

_____

_____

_____

_____

_____

_____

_____

_____

ACTION

_____

_____

_____

_____

AFFIRMATION

Caregiving has changed and affirmed my life purpose.

WRITING PROMPT

I am needed because

_____

_____

_____

_____

_____

_____

_____

_____

_____

_____

_____

_____

ACTION

_____

_____

_____

_____

DATE

AFFIRMATION

Worry can creep into my thoughts, and when it does,
I take steps to cope with it.

WRITING PROMPT

I'm concerned about

_____

_____

_____

_____

_____

_____

_____

_____

_____

_____

_____

ACTION

_____

_____

_____

_____

AFFIRMATION

Medication can make my loved one forgetful,
yet he (she) still says wise things.

WRITING PROMPT

Some of the wise things my loved one has recently said are

_____

_____

_____

_____

_____

_____

_____

_____

_____

ACTION

_____

_____

_____

_____

DATE

AFFIRMATION

*I'm always respectful of my loved one's need for
privacy and modesty.*

WRITING PROMPT

The steps I take to retain modesty are

_____

_____

_____

_____

_____

_____

_____

_____

_____

_____

_____

ACTION

_____

_____

_____

_____

_____

AFFIRMATION

Connecting with other family caregivers helps me.

WRITING PROMPT

I connect with other caregivers at

_____

_____

_____

_____

_____

_____

_____

_____

_____

_____

_____

ACTION

_____

_____

_____

_____

DATE

AFFIRMATION

I try to balance my loved one's dependence on me with
his (her) need for independence.

WRITING PROMPT

I encourage my loved one to

_____

_____

_____

_____

_____

_____

_____

_____

_____

_____

_____

_____

ACTION

_____

_____

_____

_____

DATE

AFFIRMATION

Although I think I know lots about caregiving,
it can still surprise me.

WRITING PROMPT

I'm surprised at

_____

_____

_____

_____

_____

_____

_____

_____

_____

_____

_____

ACTION

_____

_____

_____

_____

DATE

AFFIRMATION

I have prepared for health care emergencies.

WRITING PROMPT

These are the names and numbers for people to contact in case of
emergency:

_____

_____

_____

_____

_____

_____

_____

_____

_____

_____

ACTION

_____

_____

_____

_____

DATE

AFFIRMATION

*I've tried to make my loved one feel comfortable,
secure, and loved.*

WRITING PROMPT

These are some of the things I've done to help my loved one:

_____

_____

_____

_____

_____

_____

_____

_____

_____

_____

_____

ACTION

_____

_____

_____

_____

AFFIRMATION

Amidst the hustle and bustle of caregiving,
I managed to find a quiet, nurturing place.

WRITING PROMPT

My quiet, nurturing place is

_____

_____

_____

_____

_____

_____

_____

_____

_____

_____

_____

ACTION

_____

_____

_____

_____

DATE

AFFIRMATION

*I'm careful about the caregiving websites I visit,
what I click on, and what I read.*

WRITING PROMPT

These are some of my favorite websites and the reasons I visit them:

ACTION

AFFIRMATION

*I'm not afraid to revise my caregiving task list
when I feel it is necessary.*

WRITING PROMPT

This is a list of my current caregiving tasks:

_____

_____

_____

_____

_____

_____

_____

_____

_____

_____

_____

ACTION

_____

_____

_____

_____

AFFIRMATION

My dependability, no matter what happens,
is one of my caregiving strengths.

WRITING PROMPT

I can be depended on for

_____

_____

_____

_____

_____

_____

_____

_____

_____

_____

_____

ACTION

_____

_____

_____

_____

DATE

AFFIRMATION

Caregiving may well be the hardest job I've ever had in my life.

WRITING PROMPT

The challenging aspects of caregiving for me are

_____

_____

_____

_____

_____

_____

_____

_____

_____

_____

_____

_____

ACTION

_____

_____

_____

_____

_____

DATE

AFFIRMATION

> *Just as I am unique, my caregiving is unique, and I quell the urge to compare myself to other family caregivers.*

WRITING PROMPT

The unique aspects of my caregiving include

_____

_____

_____

_____

_____

_____

_____

_____

_____

_____

_____

ACTION

_____

_____

_____

_____

AFFIRMATION

Caring for my loved one is a spiritual experience.

WRITING PROMPT

Spiritual feelings come over me

_____

_____

_____

_____

_____

_____

_____

_____

_____

_____

_____

ACTION

_____

_____

_____

_____

DATE

AFFIRMATION

*Each small success my loved one achieves is
worthy of celebration.*

WRITING PROMPT

I celebrate his (her)

_____

_____

_____

_____

_____

_____

_____

_____

_____

_____

_____

ACTION

_____

_____

_____

_____

_____

AFFIRMATION

When I awaken in the morning, I think of three people
who have made my life better.

WRITING PROMPT

I am grateful to these people and for these reasons:

_____

_____

_____

_____

_____

_____

_____

_____

_____

_____

ACTION

_____

_____

_____

DATE

AFFIRMATION

My loved one's bedroom isn't a hospital room;
it is a cozy, comforting, secure place.

WRITING PROMPT

To improve my loved one's bedroom, I

_____

_____

_____

_____

_____

_____

_____

_____

_____

_____

_____

ACTION

_____

_____

_____

_____

DATE

AFFIRMATION

I do my best each day and go to bed secure in this knowledge.

WRITING PROMPT

My best efforts today

_____

_____

_____

_____

_____

_____

_____

_____

_____

_____

_____

_____

ACTION

_____

_____

_____

_____

AFFIRMATION

Helplessness is a terrible feeling, and I continue to learn how to cope with it.

WRITING PROMPT

I feel helpless when

_____

_____

_____

_____

_____

_____

_____

_____

_____

_____

_____

ACTION

_____

_____

_____

_____

AFFIRMATION

Sometimes the most special moments of caregiving
are the quietest ones.

WRITING PROMPT

In the quiet, I

_____

_____

_____

_____

_____

_____

_____

_____

_____

_____

ACTION

_____

_____

_____

_____

DATE

AFFIRMATION

To calm my soul and center my thoughts, I pray about caregiving.

WRITING PROMPT

I wrote my own caregiving prayer, and this is it:

_____

_____

_____

_____

_____

_____

_____

_____

_____

_____

_____

ACTION

_____

_____

_____

_____

DATE

AFFIRMATION

I enjoy cooking for my loved one, and I fix balanced, nutritious meals.

WRITING PROMPT

Some of my loved one's favorite meals are

_____

_____

_____

_____

_____

_____

_____

_____

_____

_____

ACTION

_____

_____

_____

_____

DATE

AFFIRMATION

Saying "no" is painful, and when I have to say it, I say it gently.

WRITING PROMPT

I said "no" to

ACTION

DATE

AFFIRMATION

When I get frustrated and upset, I spell l-o-v-e in my mind.

WRITING PROMPT

I love my loved one because

_____

_____

_____

_____

_____

_____

_____

_____

_____

_____

_____

_____

ACTION

_____

_____

_____

_____

AFFIRMATION

I include some "me time" in each caregiving day.

WRITING PROMPT

"Me time" can be

_____

_____

_____

_____

_____

_____

_____

_____

_____

_____

_____

ACTION

_____

_____

_____

_____

AFFIRMATION

*Although I've learned much about caregiving, I continue
to learn about it and how I can improve it.*

WRITING PROMPT

I've improved my caregiving by

_____

_____

_____

_____

_____

_____

_____

_____

_____

_____

ACTION

_____

_____

_____

_____

AFFIRMATION

I'm responsible for my own happiness; nobody else has that job, not family, not friends, not other caregivers.

WRITING PROMPT

Some of the things that make me happy are

_____

_____

_____

_____

_____

_____

_____

_____

_____

_____

_____

ACTION

_____

_____

_____

_____

AFFIRMATION

I've learned to be self-compassionate about caregiving.

WRITING PROMPT

I practice self-compassion

_____

_____

_____

_____

_____

_____

_____

_____

_____

_____

_____

_____

ACTION

_____

_____

_____

_____

DATE

AFFIRMATION

Joining a caregiving support group has helped me,
and I learn from other caregivers.

WRITING PROMPT

Some of the things I've learned from other family caregivers:

_____

_____

_____

_____

_____

_____

_____

_____

_____

_____

_____

ACTION

_____

_____

_____

_____

DATE

AFFIRMATION

Because caregiving can be isolating,
I make it a point to connect with others.

WRITING PROMPT

I connect with others at

_____

_____

_____

_____

_____

_____

_____

_____

_____

_____

ACTION

_____

_____

_____

_____

AFFIRMATION

I've enjoyed reading poetry and I've benefited from it.

WRITING PROMPT

This is a poem about caregiving:

_____

_____

_____

_____

_____

_____

_____

_____

_____

_____

_____

_____

ACTION

_____

_____

_____

_____

_____

AFFIRMATION

Someday my caregiving will come to an end,
and I am preparing for this time.

WRITING PROMPT

I've prepared for the conclusion of caregiving by

_____

_____

_____

_____

_____

_____

_____

_____

_____

_____

_____

ACTION

_____

_____

_____

_____

DATE

AFFIRMATION

Journaling about caregiving has become a source of comfort.

WRITING PROMPT

Some of my favorite journaling words are

ACTION

DATE

AFFIRMATION

Being still and silent helps me to know myself and understand caregiving.

WRITING PROMPT

In the silence, I've learned

ACTION

DATE

AFFIRMATION

*Sometimes I feel discouraged, and when this happens
I ask for help.*

WRITING PROMPT

My sources of help include

ACTION

AFFIRMATION

People ask me to take care of myself, and this is wise advice.

WRITING PROMPT

I take care of myself

_____

_____

_____

_____

_____

_____

_____

_____

_____

_____

_____

_____

ACTION

_____

_____

_____

_____

AFFIRMATION

Obstacles can be a sign of progress, not regression,
and that is comforting.

WRITING PROMPT

These are some of the obstacles I've overcome:

_____

_____

_____

_____

_____

_____

_____

_____

_____

_____

_____

ACTION

_____

_____

_____

_____

_____

DATE

AFFIRMATION

I give myself "high fives" for my caregiving successes.

WRITING PROMPT

I deserve "high fives" for

_____

_____

_____

_____

_____

_____

_____

_____

_____

_____

_____

ACTION

_____

_____

_____

_____

DATE

AFFIRMATION

Even though I'm a caregiver, I can learn from my loved one,
the care receiver.

WRITING PROMPT

I've learned that

_____

_____

_____

_____

_____

_____

_____

_____

_____

_____

_____

ACTION

_____

_____

_____

_____

DATE

AFFIRMATION

I'm aware of the preciousness of my caregiving days,
and I savor them.

WRITING PROMPT

These days are precious because

_____

_____

_____

_____

_____

_____

_____

_____

_____

_____

_____

ACTION

_____

_____

_____

_____

AFFIRMATION

On dark days, I light the candle of hope and keep it going.

WRITING PROMPT

I find hope in

ACTION

_____

AFFIRMATION

Most of my self-talk is positive because I make it so.

WRITING PROMPT

Some of my self-positive statements are:

_____

_____

_____

_____

_____

_____

_____

_____

_____

_____

_____

_____

_____

ACTION

_____

_____

_____

_____

DATE

AFFIRMATION

I listen attentively to what my loved one says.

WRITING PROMPT

To be an attentive listener, I

_____

_____

_____

_____

_____

_____

_____

_____

_____

_____

_____

_____

ACTION

_____

_____

_____

_____

AFFIRMATION

I am blessed to have a supportive, helpful family.

WRITING PROMPT

Family members have

_____

_____

_____

_____

_____

_____

_____

_____

_____

_____

_____

_____

ACTION

_____

_____

_____

_____

DATE

AFFIRMATION

As my caregiving days accumulate, each day is more precious.

WRITING PROMPT

This day is precious because

_____

_____

_____

_____

_____

_____

_____

_____

_____

_____

_____

_____

ACTION

_____

_____

_____

_____

_____

DATE

AFFIRMATION

Decision-making comes down to one point:
What is best for my loved one?

WRITING PROMPT

To help my loved one, I

_____
_____
_____
_____
_____
_____
_____
_____
_____
_____

ACTION

_____
_____
_____
_____

DATE

AFFIRMATION

I'm not afraid to improvise and try new things.

WRITING PROMPT

One surprising new thing

ACTION

DATE

AFFIRMATION

Learning about my loved one's illness has helped me
to be a better caregiver.

WRITING PROMPT

My loved one was diagnosed with

_____

_____

_____

_____

_____

_____

_____

_____

_____

_____

ACTION

_____

_____

_____

_____

DATE

AFFIRMATION

Staying active and fit continues to be a goal.

WRITING PROMPT

I stay fit by

ACTION

AFFIRMATION

*Laughter is part of each day, and I'm not afraid
to laugh at myself.*

WRITING PROMPT

I laughed at myself when

_____

_____

_____

_____

_____

_____

_____

_____

_____

_____

_____

ACTION

_____

_____

_____

_____

DATE

AFFIRMATION

Taking breaks from caregiving renews my energy.

WRITING PROMPT

There are many ways for me to get a break:

_____

_____

_____

_____

_____

_____

_____

_____

_____

_____

_____

_____

ACTION

_____

_____

_____

_____

DATE

AFFIRMATION

Caregiving is a journey and love is my guide.

WRITING PROMPT

During my journey, I

_____

_____

_____

_____

_____

_____

_____

_____

_____

_____

_____

ACTION

_____

_____

_____

_____

Caregiving Action Plan

Read the action steps you have written in this journal. Put a checkmark by the key steps. Now choose the ten most important steps and write them here. Pick the most important step and start working on it.

- _____

- _____

- _____

- _____

- _____

- _____

- _____

- _____

- _____

- _____

Resources

Adams, Kathleen, M.A. *Journal to the Self: Twenty-Two Paths to Personal Growth.* New York: Warner Books, Inc., 1990, p. xv, 16, 164.

Baldwin, Christina. *One to One: Self-Understanding Through Journal Writing.* New York: M. Evans and Company, Inc, 1991, p. 6, 9, 33.

Kenison, Katrina. *The Gift of an Ordinary Day: A Mother's Memoir.* New York: Grand Central Publishing, 2009, p. 207–208.

Rogers, April. "Journal Writing Tips," posted on the Scribe Time website, www.scribetime.net/journal-writing-tips/.

Scott, Elizabeth, M.S. "The Benefits of Journaling: How to Get Started," posted on the About.com website, http://stress.about.com/od/generaltechniques/ht/howtojournal.htm.

Tartakovsky, Margarita, M.S. "Tips to Start Journaling," posted on the Psych Central website, http://psychcentral.com/blog/archives/2011/04/tips-to-start-journaling/.

Also by Harriet Hodgson

- *The Family Caregiver's Guide: How to Care for a Loved One at Home*, available from WriteLife Publishing (www.writelife.com), Amazon, and bookstores.

- *Affirmations for Family Caregivers: Words of Comfort, Energy, and Hope*, available from WriteLife Publishing (www.writelife.com), Amazon, and bookstores.

- *Happy Again! Your New and Meaningful Life After Loss*, available from WriteLife Publishing (www.writelife.com), Centering Corporation (www.centering.org), Amazon, and bookstores.

- *Seed Time: Growing from Life's Disappointments, Losses, and Sorrows*, available from Centering Corporation (www.centering.org) and Amazon.

- *Alzheimer's—Finding the Words: A Communication Guide for Those Who Care*, available from John Wiley & Sons and Amazon.

- *The Alzheimer's Caregiver: Dealing with the Realities of Dementia*, available from John Wiley & Sons and Amazon.

- *101 Affirmations to Ease Your Grief Journey: Words of Comfort, Words of Hope*, available from Amazon.

- *The Spiritual Woman: Quotes to Refresh and Sustain Your Soul*, available from Centering Corporation (www.centering.org) and Amazon.

- *Writing to Recover: The Journey from Loss and Grief to a New Life*, available from Centering Corporation (www.centering.org) and Amazon.

- *Writing to Recover Journal*, available from Centering Corporation (www.centering.org) and Amazon.

- *Walking Woman: Step-by-Step to a Healthier Heart*, available from Amazon.

About the Author

Harriet Hodgson has been a freelance writer for thirty-seven years and is the author of thirty-five books. She is a member of the Association of Health Care Journalists, Association for Death Education and Counseling, and Minnesota Coalition for Death Education and Support. In addition, she is a contributing writer for the Open to Hope Foundation website, The Grief Toolbox website, and The Caregiver Space website. She has appeared on more than 180 talk shows, including blog talk radio, CBS radio, and dozens of television stations, including CNN. A popular speaker, she has given presentations at public health, Alzheimer's, and bereavement conferences. Currently, she is giving talks to community groups about caregiving and creating a happy life and a writing life. Her work is cited in *Who's Who of American Women*, *World Who's Who of Women*, *Contemporary Authors*, and other directories. Harriet lives in Rochester, Minnesota, with her husband, John. Please visit www.harriethodgson. com for more information about this busy author, grandmother, wife, and caregiver.